Milly, Molly Patchwork Quilt

"We may look different but we feel the same."

"The school fundraiser is a month away. What are we going to sell?" gasped Miss Blythe.

Milly and Molly and their friends thought for a moment.

"We'd like to make shirts," they said.

"And I'll make a patchwork quilt with all the leftover scraps of material," said Miss Blythe. "We can raffle it."

Mr. Snip was very pleased indeed. He had lots of remnants to sell.

While everyone bought just the right piece of material with their mothers' help, Alf slipped quietly home to Nan.

Alf knew Nan's purse was stretched just keeping him fed and clothed. He also knew Nan was full of cost-saving ideas.

Milly and Molly made floral shirts of purple and green.

Jack made a shirt splattered with multi-coloured spots.

Meg made her shirt of candy stripes.

Harry made a shirt covered with orange hibiscus flowers.

Elizabeth made a blue shirt with neat white trim.

Tom made his shirt with multi-coloured, horizontal stripes.

Poppy made a shirt of red polka dots.

George made a shirt of every green in the jungle.

Sophie made a shirt sprinkled with yellow daisies.

And Alf made a checked shirt from Nan's old quilt.

"It's summertime," she said. "I don't need it."

The eye-catching display of shirts and Miss Blythe's patchwork quilt caused a sensation.

In no time the coat hangers were empty.
Miss Blythe drew the raffle.

"The winner is…Nan," she announced. "You have won the patchwork quilt."

"Hooray," cried Milly and Molly and their friends.

Nan couldn't find her voice.

And Alf was lost for words!
For only Alf and Nan knew where their checked shirt had come from.